THE COMMONWEALTH AND INTERNATIONAL LIBRARY
OF SCIENCE, TECHNOLOGY, ENGINEERING
AND LIBERAL STUDIES

Joint Chairman of the Honorary Editorial Advisory Board
SIR ROBERT ROBINSON, O.M., F.R.S.
and DEAN ATHELSTAN SPILHAUS

Publisher
ROBERT MAXWELL, M.C.

PERGAMON OXFORD RUSSIAN SERIES

GENERAL EDITOR: C. V. JAMES

Background Books: II

Russian Painting and Sculpture

11th century mosaic, with 18th century
ikonostasis. *St. Sophia Kiev.*
(*By kind permission of John Faber*)

Russian Painting and Sculpture

By

MARY CHAMOT

Assistant Keeper, Tate Gallery

PERGAMON PRESS
OXFORD · LONDON · PARIS · FRANKFURT

THE MACMILLAN COMPANY
NEW YORK

PERGAMON PRESS LTD.
Headington Hill Hall, Oxford
4 & 5 Fitzroy Square, London W.1

THE MACMILLAN COMPANY
60 Fifth Avenue, New York 11, New York

COLLIER-MACMILLAN CANADA, LTD.
132 Water Street South, Galt, Ontario, Canada

GAUTHIER-VILLARS ED.
55 Quai des Grands-Augustins, Paris 6

PERGAMON PRESS G.m.b.H.
Kaiserstrasse 75, Frankfurt am Main

Library of Congress Card No. 63-19242

Set in 10 on 12 pt. Plantin and printed in Great Britain by
THE KYNOCH PRESS, BIRMINGHAM

Contents

Preface

THIS volume is one of a series of background books providing an up-to-date survey of aspects of Russian life and culture and stressing continuity from earliest times to the present day. The series is designed for all readers interested in these topics, as well as for background reading for students of Russian. It should also be of special value to potential travellers in the Soviet Union. It includes volumes on the Russian Ballet, the Russian Church, Russian Literature, Education in the U.S.S.R., and a History of Russia.

Miss Mary Chamot, the author of the present volume, was born and brought up in Russia, where she began her study of art under the well-known artist and illustrator, Kardovskii. Later she studied at the Slade School and has written and lectured on various aspects of European Art, both in Great Britain and in North America. She is the author of *Modern Painting in England*, (1937), and since 1950 has been an Assistant Keeper at the Tate Gallery in London. She has revisted Russia three times in recent years, and is one of the foremost authorities in the West on Russian art.

In her book Miss Chamot concentrates on painting but mentions sculpture where it is of outstanding interest. Because of limitations of space she does not discuss architecture or the applied arts except occasionally as a background to the development of painting.

The author would like to thank the Society for Cultural Relations with the U.S.S.R. for the loan of books, and all those friends and colleagues who have helped her in typing and reading the manuscript and proofs, as well as friends in the Soviet Union who have provided information and supplied photographs. The Editor would like to record especial thanks to Mr. Viktor Louis, Moscow, for his assistance in obtaining photographs, and to the Soviet Trade Delegation in London for permission to reproduce them. Acknowledgement is also due to M. Michel Seuphor for his kind permission to reproduce the Larionov portrait of Tatlin.

C. V. JAMES
Editor

Oxford

List of Plates

Frontispiece: 11th century mosaic, with 18th century ikonostasis. *St. Sophia, Kiev.*

Plate

Some General Characteristics of Russian Art

THE ACHIEVEMENTS of Russian painting can be fully appreciated only in Russia. Except for the works of a few twentieth-century *émigré* artists, it is almost unrepresented in European and American museums. Although up to the eighteenth century Russian painting followed a very different course from the other European Schools, it has certain affinities with English art that should help towards a better understanding. The medieval tradition lasted longer in Russia than anywhere else in Europe. As in England, there was practically no echo of the Renaissance humanist outlook, with its realistic treatment of the human figure. During the sixteenth and seventeenth centuries Russia continued to produce mainly religious art. In the eighteenth century the Western style was adopted, but only in the immediate entourage of the court.

In the nineteenth century Russia produced a number of distinguished academic painters, particularly during the early Romantic period, but showed less originality than England in landscape; later a group of genre painters reflected the day-to-day life of the people, much as the mid-Victorians did here. Parallel to the Pre-Raphaelite movement and the Gothic revival, there was a Slavic revival in Russia, which encouraged the painting of historical, legendary and religious subjects, as well as church decoration, and this eventually led to the rediscovery of the beauty of peasant and popular art. In the seventies the influence of French Realism was particularly strong among the left-wing painters, who aimed at bringing about a betterment of the people's lot. In the eighties, the new achievements of the French Impressionists began to be known in Russia, and some advanced painters became more interested in form and treatment than in subject. Paris was the centre of attraction for a coterie of artists in the nineties, who called themselves the "World of Art" (*Mir Iskusstva*); they were also influenced by Beardsley and Conder.

In the twentieth century a more revolutionary generation was quick to absorb the innovation of the Fauves, Cubists and Futurists, adding new developments such as Rayonism, Constructivism and Suprematism. After the Revolution in 1917 these *avant-garde* artists, some of whom had been working in France and Germany before 1914, flocked back to Russia, and many received important official appointments. But the new freedom of expression did not last long, and from the middle twenties the only form of painting officially encouraged was Socialist Realism. Since then there has been a great deal of production, but little development of style.

Broadly speaking, Russian art can be divided into three main periods: (1) The medieval period from the eleventh century to the end of the seventeenth, when painting was nearly always religious in character and took the form either of wall decoration or of ikon painting, in a style derived from Byzantine art; (2) the eighteenth, nineteenth and first quarter of the twentieth century, when Russian painting followed the general trend of European art; and (3) Soviet art since about 1925, when the realist narrative style of the late nineteenth century was revived and none of the modern international movements appear to have been followed. Within these periods there has been a remarkable oscillation between extreme formalism on the one hand, as in the early Russian school, and again in the golden decade of 1910–20, and intense matter-of-fact realism on the other.

Certain basic characteristics of the Russian people emerge in painting, above all their love of splendour and size. The lavish use of gold in church decoration continued later in the taste for gilt statuary to adorn the palaces and fountains of the eighteenth century. Red has always been the favourite colour in Russian, the very word is synonymous with beauty. The red shirt for men and red tunic for women was the most popular holiday attire of the Russian peasant, and red played an important part in peasant embroidery. In combination with green and yellow, white and black, it formed the basic colour scheme of some of the best ikons of the fourteenth-century Novgorod school. At a later date one of the most striking reasons for the success of Diaghilev's ballet during its first triumphs in the West was the daring colour combinations in its decor.

As in England, a strong literary trend runs through Russian painting and may account for the fact that the Russians have excelled in book illustrations, particularly in recent years. The effect on painting of Russia's close contact through the ages with the East has not yet been sufficiently explored, though the influence is apparent in the applied arts.

In portraiture the Russians have always been more successful in the rendering of character than in suggesting courtly grace or elegance, and in landscape the immense spaciousness of the country, with wide rivers and distant horizons, has naturally led to breadth and simplicity of design. Many of the domestic genre scenes are not without a touch of humour, reflecting similar trends in the theatre.

The most encouraging signs of the present day are the keen interest taken by the Russian people in the art of their country, both past and present, and the useful educational work done by the government to foster this.

CHAPTER I

Ikon Painting and Church Decoration; c.1000–1700

NO PAINTING has survived in Russia from earlier than the eleventh century, that is, from before the forcible Christianization of the people of Kiev by Prince Vladimir in 989. At this time all relics of the earlier heathen worship were swept away, and priests, craftsmen and works of ecclesiastical art were brought from Constantinople. Thus the earliest monuments in Russia, the churches of Kiev, with their frescoes and mosaics, are of the highest quality. The Cathedral of St. Sophia, though frequently rebuilt and much restored, still stands and must have served as a point of departure for the development of subsequent church architecture.

The general decoration of the Russian church is closely related to its ritual. Sculpture was never tolerated by the Eastern Church, and therefore the exterior of the buildings is usually plain stone, or brick plastered and painted white. The interior is richly ornamented with mosaic or painting. The plan of the church is generally rectangular, with three or more apses on the east side and a dome surmounting the central area, with smaller domes over the four corners. These rest on massive piers and vaults and are raised on high drums. The general impression of a Russian church, unlike a Gothic cathedral, is one of height rather than length, and this is emphasized by the painted or mosaic decorations, which carry the eye upward. A huge and highly stylized head of Christ often fills the central dome, making the worshipper instantly aware of the all-pervading deity. Below or round the other domes are ranged archangels, apostles, evangelists and saints, often set against a background of gold. In the apse stands the Virgin, with raised hands in an attitude of prayer, symbolizing the Church, and the Last Judgement sometimes occupies the west wall (Frontispiece).

In the Russian Church the celebration of mass takes place in the sanctuary behind the closed doors of the ikonostasis. By the fifteenth century this became a tall screen covered with paintings, separating the altar from the congregation. On the spandrels over the door, or, as in St. Sophia in Kiev, in the apse itself, Christ is represented giving wine to six disciples on one side, and bread on the other. The royal doors leading to the altar are usually decorated with the Annunciation and the four Evangelists. The rest of the screen is covered with ikons, varying according to the dedication of the church, but all in a strictly prescribed order. The Virgin is placed on the right of the door, the patron saint of the church on the left. Over the door is the Deisis, Christ in glory with the Virgin on his right and St. John on his left, flanked by archangels, apostles and saints. These figures are often over life size. Above them is a row of smaller pictures representing the twelve Feasts of the Church, and illustrating the principal scenes in the life of the Virgin and Christ, including the Nativity, Baptism, Raising of Lazarus, Transfiguration, Entry into Jerusalem, Crucifixion, Resurrection, Ascension, Pentecost and Assumption. The uppermost tiers are often filled with half-length figures of the prophets and the ancestry of Christ. This screen separates, as it were, the mystic consecration, which takes place in the sanctuary, from the congregation in the nave, and serves as a symbol of the celestial presence.

In general, Russian ikon painting never aims at realistic representation. Its purpose is to evoke an image and at the same time express its other-worldliness. The Church has always opposed any deviation from the traditional images based on Byzantine art. Nevertheless there was considerable development over the centuries, and by degrees Russian painters succeeded in producing a style of their own and even painted images of new local saints and historical scenes unknown in Constantinople.

The early school of Kiev flourished in the eleventh and twelfth centuries and produced, apart from mosaics and wall decorations, one of the noblest ikons to be found in Russian museums, the "Annunciation," now in the Tret'yakov Gallery. This is severely classical and somewhat austere. The full-length "Virgin Orans" in the same gallery, both her arms raised in prayer, with the Christ Child symbolized in a medallion on her breast, is more geometric in design, but gentler in expression.

A much more popular image was the "Virgin of Vladimir", probably painted in Constantinople in the eleventh century and brought to Russia soon after. It represents the most human and endearing aspect of the Virgin known in Byzantine art, the Virgin of Tenderness, so called because the Infant Christ is shown with his arms round her neck, gazing up at her while she looks dreamily beyond the spectator into space. This ikon was greatly venerated and frequently copied by Russian artists and is now in the Tret'yakov Gallery. It was named after the city of Vladimir, where it was kept from 1155 to 1395, before being transferred to the Uspenskii Cathedral in Moscow.

Vladimir and the neighbouring cities of Suzdal' and Rostov the Great became the principal centres of artistic activity in the late twelfth and early thirteenth centuries. The enlightened Prince Andrei Bogolyubskii caused churches and palaces to be erected there. Some fragments of twelfth-century frescoes in the churches of Vladimir still survive, although there has been much destruction and restoration in the course of time.

This region, to the north-east of Moscow, was ravaged by the invading hordes of Mongols in the thirteenth century, and the only important city to escape occupation was Novgorod, which continued its trade with both the East and West, amassed great wealth, and employed painters from Kiev and Constantinople to decorate its many churches. One of the earliest ikons to show markedly Russian characteristics as distinct from the Byzantine style is the large "Dormition of the Virgin", dating from the early thirteenth century. The composition expresses the joyous aspect of the event, for while the Apostles are gathered in grief round the bier, fluttering angels greet the arrival of the Virgin's soul in heaven, borne up in the arms of Christ. The colours are extraordinarily beautiful, with delicate pinks and blues, greens, reds and browns, set against a background of gold (Plate 1). In spite of the heavy damage caused by the German invasion of 1941, some buildings in Novgorod still retain traces of their original cycles of frescoes. The most important of these are the works of Theophanes the Greek, who came from Constantinople; he is recorded as having worked in the Church of the Trans-figuration in 1378, and must have brought about the great revival of Russian painting in the late fourteenth and early fifteenth centuries.

The Novgorod ikons of the fourteenth century are remarkable for their vivid colour: the background is usually vermilion, setting off strong greens and browns. St. Nicholas the Wonder-Worker was a much venerated saint and is often represented half-length, with small scenes from his life forming a border all round, as in certain thirteenth-century Italian paintings of St. Francis. The general similarity between the paintings of Novgorod and Italy may be accounted for by their common origins in Byzantine art. Later ikons were often protected and enriched by plates of silver or brass, so that only the faces and hands of the original painting remained visible. An interesting example of the beginning of this practice is seen in the painting "St. Theodore Stratelates with scenes from his Life", c. 1500, which has a background of silver repoussé as well as a narrow outer border (Plate 2).

More original is the representation of the two princes Boris and Gleb, sons of Prince Vladimir, who were slain during the inter-necine wars and became popular warrior saints. The beautiful fourteenth-century ikon in the Russian Museum, Leningrad, represents them attired in rich tunics and mantles, with fur-trimmed caps and holding swords. But for all the detail of their costumes and modelling in their faces, they lack substance and appear to hover in space as visions, appropriately ethereal.

The greatest Russian ikon painter, ANDREI RUBLEV, is first recorded as working in Moscow in the Cathedral of the Annunciation in 1405 on the earliest surviving ikonostasis together with Theophanes the Greek and a painter from Gorodets. He is probably responsible for some of the ikons in the Feast tier. Later he painted the famous "Trinity", now in the Tret'yakov Gallery for the Monastery of St. Sergius at Zagorsk (Plate 3). This is typically Russian in the mystic conception of the subject, symbolized by the three angels who appeared to Abraham and are shown round a table on which stands a chalice. The rhythmic lines and delicate colouring of this composition convey the spirituality of the theme. Rublev was also the author of a Deisis from Zvenigorod and of a number of mural paintings in the Church of the Dormition in Vladimir, where he worked with Daniil Chernyi.

As the Tartar invasion was gradually repelled in the fourteenth century, Moscow began to assume predominance over the other principalities, and by the sixteenth century Russia became unified under the Great Princes of Moscow. Painters as well as other craftsmen were naturally attracted to the capital. One of these, the painter Dionysios, may have been of Byzantine origin, like Theophanes. Ikons of the Metropolitans of Moscow, Peter and Alexis, are attributed to him. The one of Alexis is particularly beautiful in colour, with pale blues on a white ground, and the usual scenes from his life depicted with lively invention in the borders. The saint himself stands stiffly, like the earlier Virgin Orans, arrayed in splendid vestments and holding the book of Gospels in his hand. Narrative subjects showing local miracles, sometimes in several successive scenes, became popular at this period, for example the legend of the Virgin's intercession during the battle between Novgorod and Suzdal'. Elaborate scenes of the Last Judgement and of the Church Militant were also painted.

After the fire which devastated Moscow in 1547, painters were called from Novgorod, Pskov and other cities and given special quarters in the Kremlin, where with other craftsmen they formed the nucleus of the "Armoury" (*Oruzheinaya palata*) and worked exclusively for the Tsar. The name still exists to designate the enormous museum containing the magnificent collection of imperial treasure, ranging from armour to jewellery, thrones, regalia and coaches.

In the seventeenth century the Church continued to lay down rigid rules regarding ikonography and to condemn any departure from tradition, thus eliminating the possibility of free development in painting. "He who shall paint an ikon out of his imagination shall suffer endless torment", ran an injunction issued in 1658. Many ikons considered heretical were burnt after the great schism in the Russian Church, and this caused the Old Believers to make indestructible brass ikons for devotional purposes.

However, private patrons were beginning to exercise their influence, and a particularly delicate group of ikon paintings was produced for the wealthy merchants of the Stroganov family in the north-east of Russia. Small in scale, with bright colours, high finish and rich gilding, they were much admired, and their style spread to Moscow and other centres. The influence of Western art began to make itself felt through engravings and led to a more naturalistic treatment, particularly of backgrounds. The most distinguished painter of this period was SEMEN USHAKOV (1626–86), who introduced a gentler type, with more modelling in his figures than was usual in earlier ikon painting, and combined this with the fine, miniature-like treatment of the Stroganov masters. A number of painters who worked for the Tsar at this period are known by name, since they usually signed their works. No wall paintings by Ushakov have survived, but it is known that contemporary historical scenes began to make their appearance beside biblical ones.

A particularly fine series of murals has survived in Rostov and Yaroslavl', dating from the seventeenth and early eighteenth centuries. Some fifty churches in Yaroslavl' alone were covered with painting from floor to domes by bands of artists who worked with astonishing skill and rapidity, so that an entire interior would be painted in a single short summer season of about three months. Full particulars of the artists' and patrons' names are usually inscribed on the walls, and the technique employed, a combination of fresco and distemper, has retained all its freshness and brilliance. Biblical scenes, legends of saints, genealogies of ruling princes, and fanciful interpretations of the Song of Songs are the favourite subjects. Although some compositions are based on Western models, which became known in Russia through Piscator's illustrations to the Bible, published in 1650, the baroque movement of the engravings is replaced by a flat decorative pattern, and the details of architecture and costume show a lively observation of contemporary life. The best surviving examples are in the churches of St. John the Baptist and Elijah the Prophet in Yaroslavl'. These gaily painted interiors represent the last phase of the medieval Russian tradition.

Hereditary ikon painters continued to work in the region, and after the Revolution, when there was no more demand for religious painting, many of these artists took to illustrating popular folk tales on lacquer boxes. The famous Palekh work, as it is called from the village where it is produced, is executed with incredible delicacy and carries on to this day something of the inventiveness and charm of early Russian painting.

CHAPTER II

The Age of Court Patronage: c. 1700–1800

THERE HAD been few moments in the earlier history of art when a change so profound and so sudden occurred as in the reign of Peter the Great in Russia. Moreover, this was a change largely imposed by the ruler himself, and was not an evolution due to the general development of taste, as had occured in Renaissance Italy.

In the first quarter of the eighteenth century Russia, till then a little-known, backward and isolationist state, became one of the great powers of Europe. When the young Tsar returned from his tour of Western Europe in 1698, he was determined to break down the old-fashioned way of life in his native country and introduced, forcibly where necessary, the foreign customs he so greatly admired. St. Petersburg, the new capital which he founded on the Baltic, became symbolic of this changed outlook and astonished the world by the rapidity of its growth and the beauty of its design. Foreign architects, painters and sculptors were invited to come to Russia, and these left their stamp on the design of the new city. Peter was an enthusiastic collector of works of art and curios of every kind, and the treasures he amassed formed the nucleus of the Hermitage and other museums in Russia, where they have helped to cultivate taste ever since. But probably the most important measure undertaken for the development of painting was the decision to send promising young Russian artists to study abroad.

Among the first to benefit by this princely gesture were IVAN NIKITIN (c. 1690–1741), who spent five years in Venice, and ANDREI MATVEYEV (1701–39), who was sent to Antwerp in 1715 for about ten years and is best known for the attractive double portrait of himself and his wife.

The transition from ikon painting to court portraiture in the European tradition was not quite unheralded. Some of the later ikons of more or less contemporary Russian saints, such as St. Sergius of Radonezh, already expressed individuality. In the seventeenth century portraits of Tsars, boyars and ecclesiastics were sometimes painted in the ikon technique, and gradually the demand arose for more realistic portraits, or *parsuns*, as they were called. These were at first stiff and flat, like certain early Stuart portraits, though more coarsely painted, but not lacking in expression, as in the portrait of Yakov Turgenev. Nevertheless, the change from these beginnings of realistic treatment to the courtly gestures, suave technique and general competence of Matveyev and Nikitin was a surprising achievement for a single generation. Nikitin's portrait of Golovkin has all the elegance of French or Venetian portraiture of the period. But strong opposition to the new manner on the part of the clergy and the conservative nobility caused Nikitin to return to the traditional style of ikon painting, and this led to his exile to Siberia, so that little can be ascribed to him with certainty.

The reign of the Empress Elizabeth (1741–61), the Elizabethan period, as it was called in Russia, was the golden age of Russian Rococo, when Rastrelli built his magnificent palaces and churches in and around St. Petersburg, and a number of distinguished foreign painters were lured to the Northern court. They employed Russian assistants for the portraits and decorative work they were entrusted with, and thus provided an excellent training in the new style for the next generation of Russian artists.

In 1757 the Academy of Arts was founded, with an Art School where young Russians of promise received not only artistic instruction, but in the early days a general education as well, for the standard of literacy in the country was very low. The project for the Academy of Arts had been formulated in the last years of the reign of Peter the Great. At that time the craftsmen formerly attached to the Armoury in Moscow were dispersed; many were forcibly transferred to St. Petersburg and formed into working parties (*artels*). Numerous complaints testify to the miserable conditions in which they were obliged to work, while foreigners received greater privileges and far richer rewards. Among the latter, Louis Caravacque, who came to Russia in 1716 and remained until his death in 1754, enjoyed a considerable reputation as court portrait painter, and the Italian Pietro Rotari decorated a number of palaces with portraits of Elizabethan court ladies. The Russian ALEKSEI ANTROPOV (1716–95) studied with both of them and mastered the new idiom to a great extent, but without losing the power of expressing individuality and national character with a directness which sometimes recalls the qualities of American primitive portraiture of the same period.

It was Antropov who first discovered the greatest Russian painter of the century, DMITRII LEVITSKII (1735–1822), while decorating the church of St. Andrew in Kiev. Levitskii was the son of a priest, attached to the Lavra monastic printing office as engraver, and was already familiar with Western art, so that it was not difficult for him to adapt himself to the new requirements. He accompanied Antropov to St. Petersburg, continued his studies there, and developed a style of portraiture far more elegant than that of his master. His sitters appear to move freely in their courtly or domestic setting; their gestures are derived from the French court painters of the age of Louis XIV, and the artist always paid great attention to details of costume. He distinguished himself at the first exhibition held at the Academy in 1770 with the portrait of Kokorinov, the architect who collaborated with Vallin de la Mothe in erecting the building of the Academy of Arts on the banks of the Neva.

Levitskii was equally successful in painting the Empress Catherine the Great, with all the allegorical emblems demanded by that imperious lady, and the homelier portrait of the mining magnate Demidov, who posed wearing a dressing gown and night-cap and pointing to the plants he had just been watering (Plate 5).

In the Hermitage Collection, founded by Catherine, Levitskii was able to study the works of Rembrandt and Van Dyck, and he must have met a number of foreign painters who were still working in Russia, such as the Swede Roslin, and the Frenchman Tocqué. Like his contemporary, Reynolds, he tried his hand at various styles; his range may be seen by contrasting the straight-forward and penetrating portrait of his father with the many graceful and sometimes artificial-looking court ladies and actresses he portrayed. His most delightful achievement is the series of seven pictures of Catherine's favourite protégées at the Smolnyi Institute, which she had founded for the education of well-born young ladies. The girls are all dressed up and practising various accomplishments, such as dancing, reading, playing the harp and acting (Plate 4). The charm and brilliance of this group of portraits is enhanced by the splendid setting of the Mikhailovskii Palace, now the Russian Museum in Leningrad, where they are displayed together with other examples of Levitskii's work. Painted in 1773–6, they mark the period of his greatest success and favour at court. In the following decade the taste for Neo-Classicism began to prevail in Russia, and Levitskii—essentially a Rococo painter—sank into obscurity and ended his days in penury and blindness.

After the French revolution, Catherine turned her attention more and more to England in matters of taste. She already had in her employ the Scottish architect Charles Cameron, who extended and redecorated her palace at Tsarskoye Selo (now Pushkin), and she had bought pictures by Reynolds and Joseph Wright of Derby. English influence certainly prevailed during the last decade of the century. Although no painting by Gainsborough appears to have found its way to Russia at that time, his style was probably known through mezzotint engravings, and an echo of his elegant and somewhat elongated ladies can be seen in the work of FEDOR ROKOTOV (1763–1808). A substantial part of Russian society had remained in Moscow, and Rokotov spent the middle years of his career there, away from the court. His work is less ambitious in scale and design than Levitskii's, most of his portraits being head-and-shoulders with plain backgrounds. In the eighties, after his return to St. Petersburg, Rokotov's paintings became softer in colouring and more poetic in interpretation.

The most popular painter of the nineties was VLADIMIR BOROVIKOVSKII (1757–1825). A Ukrainian like Levitskii and the son of an artist, he came to St. Petersburg in 1788 and soon won favour by expressing in his painting the current wave of sentimentality and the new taste for simple life. His small scale full-length of Catherine as an old lady, taking a stroll in her park with a dog, recalls in style the earlier English conversation pieces (Plate 6), but his numerous portraits of young girls reveal a very Russian type, for all their Greuze-like posturing.

While the court portrait painters had absorbed the Western manner, both in choice of subject and in treatment, other painters, who sprang mostly from the peasantry and were actually the serfs of wealthy landowners, preferred more typically Russian scenes and retained a certain *naïveté* of style. Little is known about the painter MIKHAIL SHIBANOV except that he belonged to Prince Potemkin and appears to have had no academic training. His two pictures in the Tret'yakov Gallery, "The Peasant family at Dinner" (1774) and "The Marriage Contract" (Plate 13), are not only valuable as historical records, but show interesting powers of observation and craftsmanship, though without any trace either of the old conventions still current among ikon painters or of the new court style. IVAN ARGUNOV (1727–1802), who with other members of his gifted family belonged to the great art-patron Count Sheremet'ev, was even more accomplished, as is testified by his able portraits and his influence on other painters (Plate 9). He and his son Nikolai depicted some of the actors and actresses of Sheremet'ev's private company of players, for whom the beautiful theatre at Ostankino was built under the supervision of Argunov's younger son, Pavel.

The characteristically Russian works by these artists are more attractive, though less facile, than the academic compositions of classical and historical subjects in the grand style attempted by ANTON LOSENKO (1737–73). A Ukrainian by birth, he studied under Argunov and was then sent for further study abroad. After painting a number of religious and classical subjects, he broke new ground in 1770 with his scene from Russian history depicting "Vladimir and Rogneda", in which the theatrical gestures of the principal figures accord ill with the well-observed national character of the attendants.

Landscape painting developed more slowly. In the reign of Peter the Great the chief requirement was for topographical drawing and map-making. By far the finest artist in this class, MIKHAIL MAKHAYEV (1716–70), was commissioned to record, for a series of large double-sheet engravings, the appearance of St. Petersburg at the fiftieth anniversary of its foundation. A master of perspective, he was able to convey the spaciousness of the new capital with its fleet of vessels on the wide river and noble buildings on the banks, as well as the palaces at Peterhof, Oranienbaum and Tsarskoye Selo in their original state. For the rest, Russian landscape painters of the eighteenth century showed little originality; they were content to follow French or Italian models, and some even preferred to paint Italian to Russian scenery. FEDOR ALEKSEYEV (1753–1824), after studying in Venice, developed a pleasing topographical style and painted a series of luminous views of St. Petersburg and other Russian cities (Plate 12), but it was only in the second half of the nineteenth century that a distinctive Russian school of landscape painting arose.

The achievement of Russian sculpture in the eighteenth century was even more surprising than the rise of painting, since there was no precedent for it in the Middle Ages. The Russian Church prohibited the use of sculptured images, but Russian peasant craftsmen had been skilled in the carving of wood for ornamental purposes and in making toys. FEDOT SHUBIN (1740–1805), the son of a fisherman, was born in the north near Archangel and as a boy began carving objects of bone. After studying at the Academy and abroad, under Pigalle in Paris and Nollekens in London, he returned to Russia to become the most prolific and successful maker of portrait busts of the century. He recorded the distinguished men and women of his day in a graceful, animated fashion, avoiding the excessive restlessness of the Rococo style as well as the extremes of frigid classicism which was then coming into fashion.

Among the foreign sculptors who worked in Russia, mention must be made in the first place of Count CARLO BARTOLOMEO RASTRELLI (*c.* 1674–1744), designer of the first equestrian figure of Peter the Great and father of the great architect. In 1767 the French sculptor FALCONET (1716–91) was summoned to St. Petersburg by Catherine the Great to make the more famous figure of Peter, on a rearing horse trampling a serpent. It is set on a great block of granite and is indisputably the most impressive equestrian monument of the period in Europe.

It is thanks to the wise patronage of a few sovereigns, endowed with taste and able to command almost unlimited resources, that Russia absorbed the Western tradition and can claim an artistic heritage unique in character in the realm of eighteenth-century architecture, but distinguished also in painting and sculpture.

CHAPTER III

The Romantic Age: c. 1800–1850

THE FIRST quarter of the nineteenth century was a period of great architectural achievement in Russia. The neo-classic taste fostered by Catherine the Great became general in the reign of her grandson, Alexander I, and conformity to it was strictly enforced for private as well as public buildings, with the result that St. Petersburg received its final and characteristic aspect of a neoclassical city. In spite of certain tasteless additions of the late nineteenth century, it still remains spacious, well planned, and remarkably uniform in design. Fortunately all recent developments are situated on the outskirts and do not alter the general aspect of the centre.

The classicism favoured by Russian architects was a singularly successful adaptation of Greek ornament and proportions to the specific requirements of a northern capital, and the Russian love of colour and gilding gave it a distinctive character. The favourite combination of yellow and white, as in the Admiralty, strikes a note of gaiety. Dark groups of bronze sculpture set off the light colour schemes, which are sometimes varied to include pale green, light blue, orange or pink.

In harmony with this elegant architectural setting, classical severity was required of the sculptors employed on public monuments: thus MIKHAIL KOZLOVSKII (1753–1802), after training in Rome and Paris, designed the statue of Suvorov in conventionalized armour, while IVAN MARTOS (1754–1835) applied the heroic formula to the earlier Russian warriors Minin and Pozharskii for their monument in Red Square in Moscow.

The invasion of Russia by Napoleon and his subsequent defeat aroused a wave of strong patriotic fervour. The making of a number of statues commemorating the Russian leaders of the period was entrusted to BORIS ORLOVSKII (1793–1837), who had begun working with Italian stonemasons in Russia and continued under Thorwaldsen in Italy. A more naturalistic treatment appears in the four Horse-Tamers made in 1839 for the Anichkov Bridge by Baron PETER KLODT (1805–67).

Russian painting in the first half of the nineteenth century followed a rather different course. Although classical subjects were enjoined by the Academy, the treatment tended to be more romantic. The lure of Italy was strong, and painters were not encouraged to emulate the revolutionary tendencies of French painting. During the final stages of the Napoleonic wars, Russian armies and diplomats travelled across Europe and, as a result of these new contacts, taste became more international. The work of the principal painters, like that of the two greatest Russian poets Pushkin and Lermontov, is deeply tinged with the romantic spirit of the age.

Enormous historical or religious compositions were the fashion, and lavish state and private patronage made it possible for painters to spend as much as a quarter of a century carrying out one great picture. The most astonishing production in this category is unquestionably "The Last Day of Pompeii" (Plate 14), by KARL BRYULLOV (1799–1852). The highly gifted son of an Italian carver who had settled in St. Petersburg, Bryullov entered the Academy at the age of ten, and in 1822, on completing his training, set out for Italy with his architect brother. Five years later he paid his first visit to Pompeii and began work on his huge 21 ft. canvas. He had steeped himself in the history of the great eruption, had attended a performance of Piccini's opera on the subject, made innumerable sketches for the composition and applied all his excellent academic knowledge to the task. The picture had an enormous success, first in Rome, where it was seen by many distinguished tourists, including Sir Walter Scott and Bulwer

Lytton, who was inspired by it to write his novel, then in Paris, and finally in St. Petersburg. But Bryullov himself did not return to Russia until 1836, and then by way of Greece and Constantinople.

After the suppression of the Decembrists revolt in 1825, the atmosphere in Russia was not encouraging to creative endeavour. Bryullov was lionized and overwhelmed with commissions, but lacked the freedom he had enjoyed in Italy and was so harassed by interference and advice that the only large composition he carried out in Russia, "The Siege of Pskov", became a grief and a vexation to him and ended in confusion. His portraits, on the other hand, are full of charm, and while conforming to the requirements of society for elegance, show great variety in design: for example, "The Horsewoman" is gaily prancing towards the spectator; Countess Samoilova is shown leaving a ball with a child; Prince Golitsyn is seated in his study with a vista of rooms in the background; a group of four girls are taking a drive in a donkey cart; some boys are boating: and in all these the artist has not only characterized the individuals, but paid great attention to composition and accessories.

The other outstanding master of the period, ALEXANDER IVANOV (1806–58), set out for Italy in 1831 and soon after arriving there conceived his great work "Christ appearing to the People" (Plate 15), which was to occupy the rest of his life. Unlike Bryullov, who had concentrated largely on the composition of his "Last Day of Pompeii", depending on Raphael for balance and the Bolognese for contrasting light and shade, Ivanov spent more time on making innumerable studies of detail from nature. He was in contact with the German Nazarenes in Rome, whose new outlook on religious art also inspired Dyce and Ford Madox Brown. Like Holman Hunt, he wanted to visit the Holy Land, but was not permitted to do so. The subject he chose was the moment when St. John, while baptizing a group of people, pointed to the figure of Christ approaching in the distance; in other words, it is the coming of the Messiah. The crowd in the foreground was intended to represent all types of human beings and the full range of human emotion with which they greet this epoch-making event. The treatment of the figures and of the diffused open-air light is naturalistic, but as a composition the picture is less satisfying than many of Ivanov's smaller illustrations for the Bible, which never got beyond the stage of drawings.

The third great "machine" of the same period is the "Brazen Serpent" by FEDOR BRUNI (1799–1875). More academic and less interesting than the other two, it was begun in 1826 and not completed until 1841. Bruni's later years were mainly devoted to decorating St. Isaac's Cathedral with religious subjects.

The landscape painter SILVESTER SHCHEDRIN (1791–1830), son of a sculptor and nephew of an earlier landscape painter, spent most of this working life in Italy and is best known for his views of Naples and Sorrento.

Among the portrait painters, VASILII TROPININ (1776–1857) and OREST KIPRENSKII (1782–1836) present a contrast of styles. Tropinin derives from the eighteenth-century naturalists, and his subjects are mainly simple people. Himself a serf, freed only in 1823, he studied at the Academy and spent his working years in the Ukraine and in Moscow. He was particularly successful in painting children, as in the delightful portrait of his son (Plate 10). Kiprenskii was also the son of a serf, but became a fashionable portrait painter in literary and intellectual circles and showed greater psychological insight and a more intimate and romantic approach to his sitters. The jaunty pose of the Hussar E. D. Davydov (Plate 7), painted in 1809, reflects all the military glamour of the period; his admirable drawings record a variety of types, and in the portrait of Yekaterina Avdulina painted in Paris in 1823 he approaches Ingres in the perfection of poise and modelling (Plate 8). Kiprenskii spent the years 1816–23 in Italy, where he was styled the Russian Van Dyck, and an early portrait of his father was actually taken to be a Rubens. Not liking the reactionary political climate of Russia in the late twenties, he returned to Italy in 1828, became involved with a

PLATE 1. 13th century, Novgorod School: Dormition of the Virgin.
Tret'yakov Gallery, Moscow

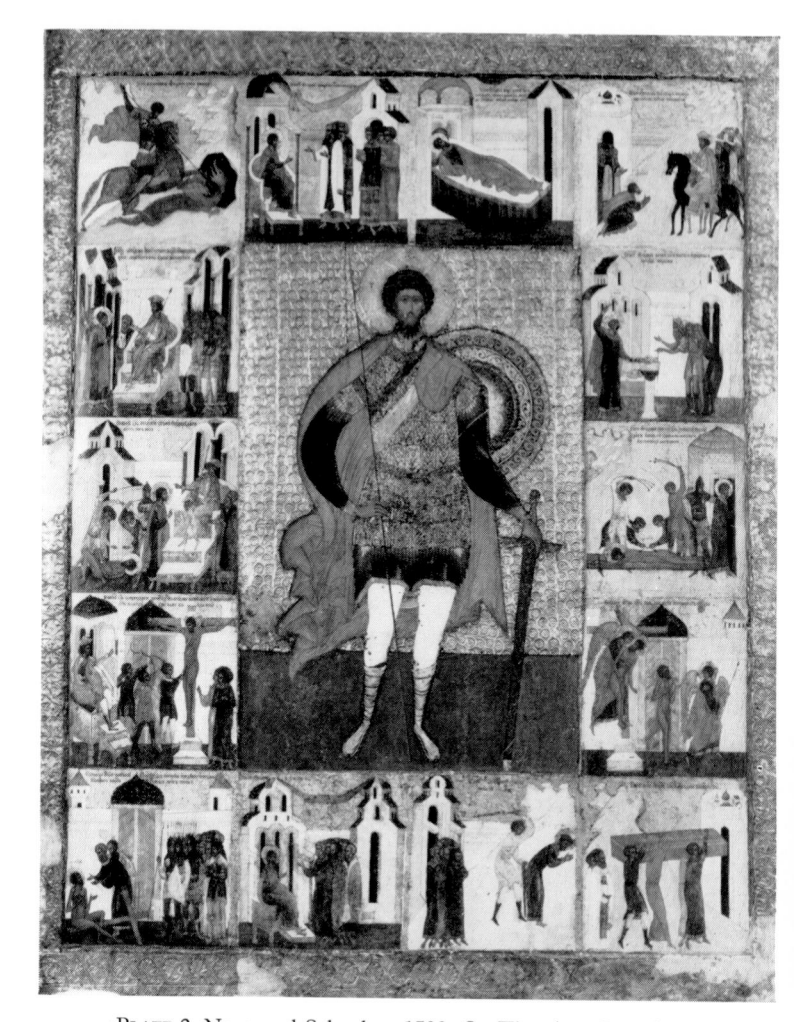

PLATE 2. Novgorod School, c. 1500: St. Theodore Stratelates.
Museum of Art and History, Novgorod

PLATE 3. ANDREI RUBLEV: The Trinity.
Tret'yakov Gallery, Moscow

PLATE 4. D. LEVITSKII: Two Smolnyi Girls Dancing.
Tret'yakov Gallery, Moscow

PLATE 5. D. LEVITSKII: Portrait of P. Demidov.
Tret'yakov Gallery, Moscow

PLATE 6. V. BOROVIKOVSKII: Catherine the Great walking in her Park at Tsarskoye Selo. *Tret'yakov Gallery, Moscow*

PLATE 7. O. KIPRENSKII: E. Davydov.
Russian Museum, Leningrad

PLATE 8. O. KIPRENSKII: Yekaterina Avdulina.
Russian Museum, Leningrad

PLATE 9. I. ARGUNOV: Woman in Russian Costume.
Tret'yakov Gallery, Moscow

PLATE 10. V. TROPININ: The Artist's Son.
Tret'yakov Gallery, Moscow

PLATE 11. A. VENETSIANOV: Peasant Girl with Calf.
Tret'yakov Gallery, Moscow

RUSSIAN PAINTING AND SCULPTURE

PLATE 13. M. SHIBANOV: The Marriage Contract. *Tret'yakov Gallery, Moscow*

PLATE 15. A. IVANOV: Christ Appearing to the People. *Tret'yakov Gallery, Moscow*

PLATE 16. A. VENETSIANOV: Harvest.
Tret'yakov Gallery, Moscow

PLATE 17. P. FEDOTOV: The Young Widow.
Tret'yakov Gallery, Moscow

PLATE 18. K. YUON: March Sun. Tret'yakov Gallery, Moscow

PLATE 19. N. GONCHAROVA: Spring Gardening. Tate Gallery, London
(Reproduced by courtesy of the Trustees of the Tate Gallery, London)

PLATE 21. V. PEROV: Troika. *Tret'yakov Gallery, Moscow*

PLATE 23. V. MAKOVSKII: On the Boulevard. *Tret'yakov Gallery, Moscow*

PLATE 24. I. REPIN: Volga Bargemen. *Russian Museum, Leningrad*

PLATE 25. V. SURIKOV: *Boyarynya Morozova. Tret'yakov Gallery, Moscow*

RUSSIAN PAINTING AND SCULPTURE

PLATE 27. M. VRUBEL': Demon. *Tret'yakov Gallery, Moscow*

PLATE 28. V. SEROV: Portrait of Princess Orlova.
Russian Museum, Leningrad

PLATE 29. M. LARIONOV: Portrait of Vladimir Tatlin.
Coll. Michel Seuphor, Paris

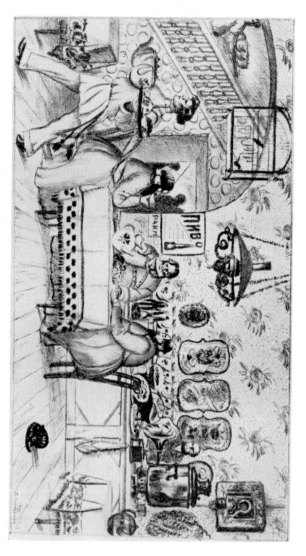

PLATE 30. B. KUSTODIEV: The Bar. (Lithograph)

PLATE 31. S. S. KONENKOV: Self-Portrait (marble). *Tret'yakov Gallery, Moscow*

PLATE 33. M. SAR'YAN: Lalvar, 1952. *Tret'yakov Gallery, Moscow*

PLATE 35. A. DEINEKA: A Relay Race. *Tret'yakov Gallery, Moscow*

PLATE 36. A. USHIN: Illustration to a poem by Sergei Yesenin

young woman, took to drink, and died of a chill contracted while sleeping out of doors.

The most typically Russian painter of this generation was ALEKSEI VENETSIANOV (1780–1847), the painter of country scenes and peasant types, whose works reveal little reference to contemporary trends in European painting. His pictures show the vast, flat landscape of central Russia, the golden light, the ripe corn and the quiet dignity of the peasant women (Plates 11 and 16). The originality of his outlook may be partly accounted for by the fact that he never attended the Academy, but had some private instruction from Borovikovskii and learned mainly by copying old masters in the Hermitage. After the censorship had prohibited the publication of his early caricatures, he turned to portraiture and in 1818 retired to his small estate at Safonkovo near Tver' (now Kalinin), where he proceeded to paint quiet interiors like "Morning", showing his wife and two peasant women, or the "Threshing Barn". Here he also started a school of his own, and trained a number of painters to work from nature in a manner opposed to the current practice of the Academy; this group produced a spate of pleasant, intimate genre scenes, interiors and landscapes.

In the forties a new element was introduced into genre painting by PAVEL FEDOTOV (1815–52), who started as an amateur and eventually gave up his career of army officer in order to devote himself entirely to painting. He was probably acquainted with the work of Hogarth through engravings and, like his English prototype, invented his own dramatic situations and was constantly observing life in its smallest details in order to collect material for his pictures. His subjects are much less violent and full-blooded than Hogarth's, and his technique is smoother, as is only to be expected in the more refined mid-nineteenth century. Nor is there any moralizing intention behind them; Fedotov's aim is rather to make a humorous commentary on the absurdities of middle-class life. A typical example is the pair of drawings illustrating the commotion caused by the sickness and death of a lady's pet dog. His attitude to human weaknesses, mildly satirical yet full of tenderness, can be compared to that of his literary contemporaries Krylov and Gogol'. The theme of one of Fedotov's most celebrated pictures, "The Major's Courtship", is basically the same as that of Hogarth's "Marriage à la Mode"—an impoverished nobleman courting a rich merchant's daughter—but the artist has confined himself to one scene, which shows the bride trying to escape when everything is set for her betrothal (Plate 20). The poignancy of a given moment is also the subject of "The Aristocrat's Breakfast"—in which the arrival of an unexpected guest causes a young man to hide the crust of bread he is eating in his elegant apartment. To drive the point home, Fedotov was in the habit of writing explanations for his pictures, sometimes in verse, and would even stand in front of them at the Academy exhibitions, declaiming his amusing jingles. The public was delighted and crowded round so as not to miss a single detail. After a surfeit of classical and religious subjects, it was a relief to the people of Russia to be able to recognize themselves and their foibles. Wilkie, Mulready and Frith enjoyed a similar success in England, but their style was more light-hearted and their colour brighter. The note of sadness became more apparent in the last years of Fedotov's short career. His "Young Widow" (Plate 17) was so popular that he had to paint several versions; a grim view of the future he feared to be in store for him inspired "The Painter's Old Age", and the futility of life was the theme of his last work, "Encore", in which a young officer in a dreary billet is amusing himself by making a little dog jump over a stick. In 1852 Fedotov lost his reason and died a few months later in an asylum, but his art had prepared the way for the critical realism of the second half of the century.

CHAPTER IV

Realist Tendencies: c. 1850–1900

AT A TIME when great innovations in the visual arts were being developed in France by a generation of pioneers who discovered a new way of seeing, as well as of painting, their Russian contemporaries were more concerned with literary subject matter and the sociological impact of their pictures.

The new political reforms culminated in the liberation of the serfs in 1861, but after the assassination of Alexander II in 1881 a period of repression set in, during which the liberal-minded intelligentsia, to which most artists belonged, used every means to stress the hard lot, ignorance and poverty of the people in contrast to the growing affluence of the ruling classes. In these circumstances it is not surprising that every picture had to present a burning problem, if not actually to preach revolt or to expose existing evils. Since the Revolution, Russian art historians have naturally emphasized this particular aspect of nineteenth-century painting, claiming a degree of originality for Russian ideological or critical realism, as it was called, which is hardly borne out by a comparison with other schools. In England there were also the Victorian moralists and realists. Pictures such as "Toil and Pleasure" by J. R. Reid, "Applicants for Admission to a Casual Ward" by Luke Fildes, "Newgate—Committed for Trial" by Frank Holl, "On Strike" by Herkomer, "Hopeless Dawn" by Frank Bramley and "The Pool of London" by Vicat Cole were all painted between 1874 and 1890. But in Russia, where the masses were more repressed and reforms more difficult to achieve, the social problem loomed larger, and there was no middle-class society to buy the type of frivolous story picture which filled the walls of the English Royal Academy during those years.

A direct follower of Fedotov, the first satirist of the social order was VASILII PEROV (1833–82). Trained in the Moscow School of Art, he struck out as a daring independent in one of his first pictures, "A Village Religious Procession at Easter" (1861), by depicting drunken priests and disorderly peasants. The picture was withdrawn from exhibition, but this did not prevent Perov from following it up with others, revealing corruption in monasteries. Most of his pictures are drily painted in drab colours, which add to the sense of desolation. The drooping lines of "The Village Burial" still further accentuate this feeling of gloom.

Two years spent in Paris on a travelling scholarship in the early sixties do not seem to have influenced Perov's style, and he hastened back to Russia to continue painting the subjects he knew best and felt most deeply about. "Troika", a group of children dragging a barrel of water on a sledge, has charm and force without sentimentality (Plate 21). A touch of humour enlivens his pictures of country types, such as "The Angler" and the "Shooting Party at Rest" (1871). Among his portraits, those of the writers Dostoyevskii and Ostrovskii show penetrating characterization.

In view of the popular success of the new topical scenes of everyday life, students were beginning to rebel at the conventional subjects set by the Academy, and in 1863, the year of the *Salon des Refusés* in Paris, a group of thirteen students left the Academy Schools as a protest at having to paint "A Feast in Valhalla", which they felt was completely divorced from real life. The leader of this group was IVAN KRAMSKOI (1837–87). His introduction to painting had been via a photographer's studio, where he had learnt to retouch and capture likenesses. Even after a brief spell at the Academy he continued to emulate the unselective fidelity of the camera. The team of young rebel artists who all lived together, and worked while Kramskoi read to them, found a patron in the rich Moscow merchant Tret'yakov. He began to buy their works, and formed the vast collection which he presented in 1892 to the city of Moscow with the gallery which still bears his name.

As they felt the need of showing their work to a wider public than could be found in Moscow and St. Petersburg, the group organized a large exhibition in 1865 during the annual fair at Nizhnii-Novgorod. The success of this venture led to a further development of travelling exhibitions and the foundation in 1870 of the Society for Travelling Art Exhibitions, known as *Peredvizhniki* (often translated as *Wanderers*). It was part of the general endeavour among the intelligentsia to bring culture to the people, and the style of painting shown was therefore popular, easily understood, literal rather than imaginative in content, and photographic rather than pictorial in treatment. The kind of realism in vogue in the seventies was something new at the time, dealing with scenes of everyday life, finding subjects in toil or simple domestic indoor and outdoor scenes, often comprising large crowds of people. Some of the painters who belonged to the society were highly gifted, but the type of painting they practised is now so out of fashion and so seldom seen in the West that it is difficult for us to approach the Russian masters with an unbiased mind.

Apart from a number of fine portraits, including a famous early one of Tolstoi, Kramskoi is chiefly remembered for his subject pictures, such as the haunting "Inspection of an Old House", "Inconsolable Grief", and "Christ in the Wilderness". There is nothing sanctimonious about this rugged figure sitting in deep perplexity in the bare rocky landscape. The artist himself declared that he had wished to express the human struggle between surrender to evil and self-sacrifice.

Religious subjects were also the chief preoccupation of the painter NIKOLAI GAY (1831–94), who was still more unconventional, and even brutal, in his interpretations of "The Last Supper", "Golgotha" and the enigmatic "What is Truth?", in which the figure of Pilate is confronted with that of Christ. Even before his close friendship with Tolstoi, Gay spent some time in seclusion, living like a peasant, but he returned to painting in 1880. The study of light-effects plays an important part in many of his pictures, ranging from the moonlight of "Gethsemane" to the glare of "Golgotha", and his treatment became more violent in his later works. One of his most accomplished and popular works is the historical scene of Peter the Great questioning his son Aleksei, in which the juxtoposition of the two characters, the autocratic father and his weakling son, is dramatically expressed.

Most of the *Peredvizhniki* were painters of genre, who preferred to depict scenes from the life of the villages or small towns they knew best. Patriotic subjects and ideological content were among the tenets insisted on by the members of the society and encouraged by the critic Stasov, who supported them. The result is a large number of paintings of great historical interest, in that they depict a way of life that no longer exists. At the time they helped to stimulate discontent with the existing order, just as the poet Nekrasov did in his famous poem "Who can live happily in Russia?". But there is little artistic merit in most of these paintings, and Alexander Benois has rightly described the seventies and eighties as "the dreariest period in the history of Russian painting". Typical examples are the works of VLADIMIR MAKOV-SKII (1846–1920), "On the Boulevard" (Plate 23), and "The Failure of the Bank"; NIKOLAI YAROSHENKO (1846–98), "The Stoker", "The Student" and "The Prisoner"; KONSTANTIN STAVITSKII (1844–1905), "Off to the War" and "Repair on the Railway". The titles alone suffice to indicate the realistic, descriptive works, which are so much vaunted today as forerunners of Soviet painting.

There is more incisive observation, crispness of handling and variety of theme in the paintings by VASILII VERESHCHAGIN (1842–1904), who was not a member of the *Peredvizhniki*. Starting as a war reporter, he travelled widely in Central Asia, India, Tibet, Western Europe and America and was killed in an explosion on a battleship in Port Arthur. His reputation was world-wide and he held successful exhibitions in Paris and London. One of his most famous works is the pyramid of skulls entitled "Apotheosis of War".

The two outstanding painters of the period, Repin and Surikov, are remembered mainly for their historical subjects. Both were bulwarks of the *Peredvizhniki* and are highly honoured in Russia today. ILYA REPIN (1844–1930) was born in the Ukraine, began working with an ikon painter, then studied under Kramskoi and entered his team (*artel'*). In 1871 he won a gold medal for his "Raising of Jairus's Daughter". While still a student at the Academy he began his great picture "The Volga Bargemen", and he and the landscape painter Vasil'yev spent the summer of 1870 painting on the Volga. Both were impressed by the spaciousness of the landscape, and Repin got to know the bargemen, tramping for miles with them before completing the studies for his picture. Few people who heard Chaliapin sing the famous "Song of the Volga Boatmen" realized the gruelling conditions of their toil as revealed by Repin. The diagonal line of the figures, dragging the heavy barge in the distance, moves as a dark mass, slowly and endlessly against a luminous background of sky and water (Plate 24). The picture had an immediate success and was exhibited in Vienna in 1873. Repin himself visited Paris that year, but the influence of open-air and impressionist painting did not deter him from pursuing the national style. He returned to his native Chuguyev and eventually painted a huge composition embodying all the village types he had studied there in "The Religious Procession in the Province of Kursk". The composition lacks the unity and power of "The Bargemen", as the figures are more spread out. Like Frith's "Derby Day", it is a picture that invites looking into, bit by bit, to discover the wealth of characterization; but there is more atmosphere, suggesting a dusty road on a hot day.

At the same time Repin was trying his hand at many other subjects; the least successful was his excursion into the realm of the fairy tale "Sadko". As a painter of history he produced among other works the violently dramatic picture of Ivan the Terrible's remorse after murdering his son, and the rollicking fun of the "Zaporozhtsy" Cossacks, the result of a detailed study of national types. Innumerable oil sketches done direct from nature, and vivid drawings of details, show his method of work and the sharpness of his observation.

He recorded many of his contemporaries in his portraits, most frequently Lev Tolstoi and members of his own family, but one of his most astonishing achievements is the enormous painting of the Jubilee Session of the Council of State (1901–3), for which he painted separate studies of all the statesmen and then managed to combine the whole in an interesting composition dominated by the festive colours of the court uniforms. It is rare for an official commission to be executed with such obvious delight and success.

In contrast to the many-sidedness of Repin's work, his contemporary, VASILII SURIKOV (1848–1916), was completely dedicated to the then fashionable form of history painting, with correct reproduction of costume and setting. His most famous works include "The Morning of the Execution of the Streltsy", a vast concourse of people on Red Square, Moscow, with Peter the Great commanding the shooting of his former bodyguard; "Men'shikov at Berezov", an interior depicting the fallen favourite in exile with his three daughters; "Yermak conquering Siberia" and, the most impressive of all, "Boyarynya Morozova", a winter scene with the fanatical black figure being driven away in a sleigh to her trial for supporting the Schism in the Church, while the populace looks on with mixed feelings, some praying, others mocking (Plate 25). In all his pictures Surikov chose a dramatic moment and expressed violent emotions, but used visual means and original compositions to convey the situation. Morozova's raised arm contrasts with the horizontal mass of the people, and the movement of the sleigh away from the spectator is emphasized by the boys running alongside. It has been said that it was the sight of a crow alighting in the snow that first gave the artist the idea for his design. As he was born and bred in Siberia, the subject of Yermak naturally appealed to him, but the treatment is confused, and the same is true of the grim picture of Suvorov's army slithering down a precipice while crossing the Alps.

Historical painting of a less dramatic type appears in the legendary subjects chosen by VIKTOR VASNETSOV (1848-1926). In the reign of Alexander III a strong Slavophile movement arose, accompanied by a revival of Orthodoxy, which brought about a demand for church decoration in a pseudo-Byzantine manner, as far removed from the real thing and as full of nineteenth-century sentimentality as was Victorian neo-Gothic. Vasnetsov decorated the church of St. Vladimir in Kiev and painted the popular picture of three legendary medieval warriors scanning the countryside for possible enemies. Reproductions of this painting were extensively used during the German invasion of 1941 to bolster up morale.

A more elegant and lyrical form of medievalism inspired the early work of MIKHAIL NESTEROV (1862-1942) in such works as "The Anchorite" and "The Vision of the young Bartholomew". The typically Russian landscape is sensitively and decoratively treated, and the figures seem to hover in space with an air of mystical solemnity like those of certain early ikons. This deeply religious mood has been severely criticized by Soviet historians, and after the revolution Nesterov painted nothing but portraits. However, a retrospective exhibition of his work was held at the Academy in Leningrad in 1962.

In contrast to all these nationalist and Slavophile painters, a group of accomplished academicians continued to paint classical subjects in an empty theatrical manner. The most successful of these was HENRY SEMIRADSKII (1842-1902) who, like Alma-Tadema, loved to paint the nude against white marble and blue sea and had an opportunity of doing this with grandiose illusionistic effect in the enormous picture of "Phryne on the Feast of Poseidon". He also tackled religious subjects in the same style, and it is interesting to compare his treatment of "Christ and the

Adultress" with a painting of the same subject by Polenov (both in the Russian Museum, Leningrad). VASILII POLENOV (1844–1927) was mainly a landscape painter, and his early work, "A Moscow Courtyard" (1878), showed that he was already acquainted with the sunlight and atmospheric effects achieved by the plein-airists and early impressionists, but he managed to combine this with a more formal design. He had painted in Normandy during his student days and later visited Greece, Syria, Palestine and Egypt, which enabled him to get a convincing setting for his religious themes.

During the second half of the nineteenth century a type of landscape painting was evolved in Russia as national as that which Constable had created earlier in England. The marine painter IVAN AIVAZOVSKII (1817–1900) was one of the first to achieve great fame for his pictures of the Black Sea, in sunlight and moonlight, storm and calm (Plate 22). IVAN SHISHKIN (1832–98) specialized in forest scenes, rendered with illusionistic precision of detail; ARKHIP KUINDZHI (1842–1910) employed a more generalized formula and was therefore able to stress light effects in a manner that appeared revolutionary at the time. However, the most typically Russian masters were ALEKSEI SAVRASOV (1830–97) and his pupil ISAAK LEVITAN (1860–1900). Savrasov's picture "The Rooks have Come" epitomizes the end of a long winter in the grey pools of melting snow and the fluttering movement of the birds in the birch trees, through which a church and belfry are seen in the distance. Levitan painted a sunny winter scene, "March", but generally preferred the green and gold of summer and autumn. His pictures are often built up on horizontal lines expressing the great plains of Russia, broken by large areas of water reflecting the sky. He used the impressionist's palette of pure colours, and combined a rendering of the clear Russian light with a delicate poetic feeling in such pictures as "Evening Bells" (Plate 26) and "Above Eternal Rest"—an old chapel and churchyard on the bank of the Volga. These pictures are carefully planned compositions, not fragments of vision, as were some of

the French impressionist works, and the artist was obviously concerned with the particular locality and its emotional significance
and found a new artistic formula in which to express these. He
was the first Russian artist to pay more attention to the quality of
painting than to the choice of subject, and thereby inaugurated
the modern period which was to produce important developments in the next decades.

CHAPTER V

Modern Movements: c. 1890–1924

THE TWO great precursors of all that is best in early twentieth-century Russian painting were Serov and Vrubel'. Both were highly gifted and developed on original lines after studying together at the Academy under Chistyakov. VALENTIN SEROV (1865–1911) was the son of a composer who died when the boy was only six years old. His mother, also a musician, travelled around Europe, and the young painter spent his childhood in Munich, Paris, Rome and Kiev in circumstances very different from those of most other Russian painters. In Paris he met Repin, who gave him private tuition until he was old enough to enter the Academy. Serov's first great success was the picture known as "The Girl with Peaches", painted at Abramtsevo in 1887, a delightfully fresh and spontaneous study of a sunlit room, with the daughter of the house, Vera Mamontova, seen against the window.

Abramtsevo, an estate near Moscow now preserved as a museum, played an outstanding part in the development of Russian art during the last three decades of the nineteenth century. The railway magnate, Savva Mamontov, was a lavish patron of the arts and used to invite the foremost painters, sculptors, musicians and actors to spend the summer at his house, where they were free to work and enjoy their host's and each other's company. Among the painters who availed themselves of this hospitality were Polenov, Repin, Vasnetsov, Kramskoi, Surikov, Nesterov, the Korovin brothers, and Vrubel'; the sculptors Antokol'skii, the singer Chaliapin, the producer

Stanislavsky and many other celebrities were also frequent visitors. Mamontov had his private theatre, for which some of the famous Russian operas by Mussorgsky and Rimsky-Korsakov were written; Vasnetsov and Korovin designed scenery and costumes for these first productions. Thus began that close co-operation between painters and the theatre which led in the twentieth century to the grandiose spectacles staged by Diaghilev.

Mamontov's personal taste, wide culture and exuberant energy left a lasting impression on the artistic life of Russia. It was at Abramtsevo that peasant crafts first began to be studied and collected, and this was to be an important factor in subsequent developments. Studios, a log hut, a bath house, a church and other buildings in the neo-Russian style were erected on the estate by Vasnetsov, who also designed the Tret'yakov Gallery in Moscow.

The end of the nineteenth century was a period of great intellectual activity; the new bourgeois society held advanced views, travelled abroad, collected with zeal and sometimes with extraordinary foresight. While Pavel Tret'yakov confined himself to buying contemporary Russian pictures, his brother collected French painting, chiefly of the Barbizon school. A little later the two adventurous merchants Morozov and Shchukin assembled the finest collections of Impressionist, Post-impressionist and Fauve paintings to be found anywhere in the world. After the Revolution these collections were nationalized, and they are now divided between the Pushkin Museum in Moscow and the Hermitage in Leningrad. But even when they were still in the private houses of their owners many artists had access to them, so that the latest developments in Paris were known in Moscow. It is not surprising that around the turn of the century Russian art ceased to be the provincial outpost of the great European tradition, as it had been since the eighteenth century. On the eve of the Revolution it rose rapidly to a position of leadership only to be set back shortly afterwards and forced to produce a rehash of the so-called "realism" of the seventies.

Influences from abroad were absorbed with such rapidity that it is impossible to classify Russian painters into the familiar categories of the various "*isms*". Many of them experimented with a variety of forms, while retaining their own individuality. Thus Serov's early work may be described as impressionist, while his latest, for instance "The Rape of Europa", and the portrait of Ida Rubinstein, shows the decorative design and distortions of the Fauves. His drawings, notably the poster of Pavlova dancing and the illustrations to Krylov's fables, are masterpieces of expression in the fewest possible lines. His historical composition of "Peter the Great" striding along, his gigantic figure silhouetted against the sky, is just as novel for the period, in being seen from below, as is the spacing of his dramatic sketch of soldiers ordered to shoot civilians during the 1905 rising, where the charging horsemen are seen from above.

A similar inventiveness appears in his many portraits. A momentary gesture or a characteristic twist of the figure would suggest a pictorial arrangement to the painter; his handling has the breadth and freshness of Manet—the silvery colour scheme is sometimes broken by emphatic contrasts of colour and tone— and in his many society portraits he conveys the elegance of his sitters and their setting without any personal flattery (Plate 28). His paintings are an epitome of upper class life and taste in pre-revolutionary Russia, the period corresponding to the Edwardian era in England, for in spite of his liberal views he was sought after by the court and carried out official and private commissions with equal unconventionality. One of his portraits of the late Emperor Nicholas II belongs to the Scots Greys Regiment.

In contrast to Serov's search for the happier aspects of life, the work of MIKHAIL VRUBEL' (1856–1910) bears the stamp of a troubled spirit. After completing his studies he embarked in 1884 on the great scheme of restoring and decorating the monastery of St. Cyril in Kiev. The study he was able to make there of medieval Russian art fired his imagination, and he produced a series of violently expressive religious compositions. The authorities were shocked by his departure from the flaccid conventions which had debased religious painting in the nineteenth century, and in 1887 he was not permitted to realize his second cycle of biblical subjects, designed for the Cathedral of St. Vladimir in Kiev. He turned to literary themes, folklore and portraits, and experimented in sculpture and theatrical decoration. The pervading image of his later work is the tragic, lonely "Demon" of Lermontov's poem (Plate 27). Vrubel's gigantic forms sometimes recall Bourdelle; allegorical treatment was in the air at the time when Watts and Böcklin were painting, but his handling is broader than theirs and his colour more broken in its prevailing cold blue and violet tones. Some of his later drawings show an emphasis on planes clearly derived from Cézanne, and many of his forms tended to squareness long before Cubism came into being. He belonged to the generation of the symbolists, a poetic movement which had a considerable following in Russia, and his influence as a painter was widespread. Another important figure, VIKTOR BORISOV-MUSATOV (1870–1905), created a world of gentle nostalgic visions in pale colours akin to that of Maurice Denis. A melancholy mood and decorative treatment were fashionable in the nineties. A different aspect of Nabi influence is apparent in the work of the Russian intimist LEONID PASTERNAK (1862–1945), father of the poet Boris. After 1921 he worked in Berlin and ended his days in Oxford.

A number of painters were turning more and more to the West for inspiration and could find no outlet for their works in the narrowly nationalist *Peredvizhniki* or the conventional Academy. In 1899 a new Society was formed, under the title *Mir Iskusstva* ("The World of Art"). It organized exhibitions and published a journal under the same name, which was at first financed by Princess Tenishev and by Mamontov. This new movement was centred mainly in St. Petersburg, and there was some rivalry, not to say antagonism, between that city and Moscow. However, in the end Serov, Nesterov, Levitan, Vasnetsov, Korovin and Golovin joined "The World of Art". The first exhibition was opened in the splendid setting of the Stieglitz Museum early in 1898 under the title "Russian and Finnish Artists", and the following year the journal *Mir Iskusstva* came out with the avowed purpose of breaking the provincialism of Russian art, arousing interest in current trends abroad and inviting foreign artists to exhibit in Russia. The leaders of the coterie that ran both the journal and subsequent exhibitions had already become friends in their school days, and all had studied abroad. They were steeped in the fashions of the nineties, had a nostalgic admiration for the eighteenth century and a profound dislike for the didactic attitude of the *Peredvizhniki*. "Art for Art's Sake" was the new slogan. Beauty of form and style were extolled, rather than meaning and purpose in painting, and in the journal the writers were often violent in attacking their opponents.

One of the prime movers of this new school was ALEXANDER BENOIS (1870–1960), the son of an architect, Nicholas Benois, whose father had come to Russia from France in 1794. The family had long-standing connections with the theatre, for which Alexander had a passion from childhood. His remarkable visual memory aided him as an art historian. He published portfolios on *The Art Treasurers of Russia* (1901–7) and wrote a *History of Russian Painting* in 1904. He and Diaghilev became close friends and collaborators, both in directing the journal and in organizing exhibitions, and eventually in the magnificent productions of the Russian Ballet. Benois's first and most memorable production was *Petrushka*, followed, among other things, by *Pavillon d'Armide*, *The Nightingale*, and *The Nutcracker*.

As a painter, Alexander Benois worked mainly in watercolours or gouache, depicting his beloved Versailles, and painting fancy pictures of old St. Petersburg and views of Peterhof with the palaces and fountains he knew so intimately, having been brought up there when his father was court architect. He was also a prolific illustrator. After the Revolution he became curator of paintings at the Hermitage, but in 1928 he settled in Paris where he spent the rest of his life, working mainly for the theatre.

LEON BAKST (1866–1925) made a still more spectacular impact with the exotic costumes he designed for Diaghilev's *Sheherazade*, for example, and he used to repeat them with great success for exhibition purposes. Sumptuous colour and a suggestion of remote antiquity in the ruggedness of his design distinguished the work of NIKOLAI ROERICH (1874–1947), who often chose scenes from Russian legends and treated them with broad decorative effect. An example of his work can be seen in the Ashmolean Museum in Oxford, the only collection in England apart from the Tate where a small nucleus of modern Russian art is to be found. Roerich's designs for *Prince Igor* successfully combined the strain of old Russian tradition and Eastern glamour with a modern interpretation, as suggested by Borodin's music.

Like Benois, KONSTANTIN SOMOV (1869–1939) was enamoured of the graces of the eighteenth century and was also fond of dreaming of the romantic eighteen-thirties. His style is more precise, his people resemble porcelain figurines, his colours are gay and crisp. He was a delicate draughtsman and excelled in illustration.

While some members of the "World of Art" movement, like KONSTANTIN KOROVIN (1861–1939), looked to Paris and introduced an echo of Impressionism into Russia, others turned their attention mainly to a revaluation of earlier Russian architecture, introducing a form of romantic topography peculiar to this movement. Under the influence of the Japanese print, ANNA OSTROUMOVA-LEBEDEVA (1871–1955) produced a series of remarkably beautiful drawings and colour prints of St. Petersburg, in which the classical buildings seem to lend themselves to new and exciting decorative arrangements. YEVGENII LANCÉRÉ (1875–1946) and GEORGII LUKOMSKII (1881–1956) were also mainly concerned with architectural evocations. MSTISLAV DOBUZHINSKII (1875–1957) divided his talents between urban landscapes, book illustrations and designs for the theatre. Though he did some designs for the ballet, his quiet and serious approach was better suited to the dramatic theatre. For many years he worked for the

Moscow Art Theatre, and after 1924 lived in Lithuania, Western Europe and finally America, where he died. ALEXANDER GOLOVIN (1863–1930), who had begun making theatre designs for Mamontov, won his greatest success with the decor for *Ruslan and Lyudmila* in 1900. IVAN BILIBIN (1876–1942) did occasional sets for the theatre, but made his chief contribution as an illustrator of fairy tales, in which text and illustrations formed a decorative whole with a typically Russian flavour.

The *Mir Iskusstva* journal ceased to exist in 1904, when the pioneers felt that they had sown the seed of new ideas. In fact it was followed by a succession of other art journals and exhibition societies, becoming gradually more and more advanced in their views. Foreign artists, including Picasso and Matisse, were invited to exhibit with the "Blue Rose" in 1907 and the "Golden Fleece" in 1908–9, and all this helped to prepare the way for the much more original generation of artists who came to the fore during the second decade. Modern developments in Russia always went hand in hand with a deeper understanding and appreciation of the past. Thus it is characteristic that Diaghilev should have first made his name by writing a book on Levitskii (1902), before organizing in 1905 the greatest exhibition of Russian historical portraits ever held. His next venture was to exhibit a representative collection of Russian painting from the eighteenth to the twentieth century at the Salon d'Automne in Paris in 1906; finally, from 1908 he introduced to the Western world splendid combinations of all the arts in his productions of opera and ballet.

In 1914 Diaghilev invited the most advanced painter in Russia, Goncharova, to design décor for his ballet. She and Larionov boldly rejected the old-fashioned antiquarianism of the "World of Art" and found their inspiration in the vigorous traditions of popular art, ikon painting, peasant toys, painted signs and embroideries. MIKHAIL LARIONOV (b. 1881) played an important part in organizing the "Golden Fleece", "Knave of Diamonds", "Donkey's Tail" and other exhibitions of *avant-garde* artists, and invented Rayonism in about 1911. This was the first step towards abstraction and was achieved by projecting lines or rays into space (Plate 29). Earlier Larionov had painted enchanting primitive scenes of provincial life and, during his military service, 1908–9, a series of pictures of soldiers. NATALYA GONCHAROVA (1881–1962) was more prolific and varied in her achievements. Eastern art and ikon painting combined to influence her decorative and religious compositions, flower pieces and scenes of colourful peasant life (Plate 19). Her rayonist works never became entirely abstract, and she used futurist methods to express the movement of machines. Her dazzling décor for *Coq d'Or* and the *Firebird* were unsurpassed in splendour and expressive colour. Both artists left Russia in 1915 and settled in Paris, attracting, until recently, far less attention than they deserved.

MARC CHAGALL (b. 1887) enjoyed a wider reputation and has scored a new triumph in recent years with his designs for stained glass. Born of a poor Jewish family in the ghetto at Vitebsk, he grew up among cows, donkeys, fish, cocks and hens, which form recurrent themes in his pictures. During his first period of study in Paris 1910–14, and his subsequent residence abroad after 1922, he continually returned to the subject of his native suburb and captured the spirit of the place with the same devotion that inspired Stanley Spencer to paint his pictures of Cookham. This profound nostalgia for the intimate family life, with its Jewish ritual and fiddle-playing uncles astride log-huts, is interspersed with day-dreams of lovers flying in ecstasy above the scene, all of which he has described in his autobiography *Ma Vie*. After the Revolution he was put in charge of art education in Vitebsk, did some decorations for Meyerhold's Jewish theatre in Moscow, and finally returned to France when he realized that there was no future for modern tendencies in Russia.

The same fate eventually befell VASILII KANDINSKY (1866–1944), the most important pioneer of abstract art. His background was very different. In the course of his studies of law and economics he had the opportunities of travelling to remote parts of

Russia and, like others of his generation, discovered the wealth of folk art there. In 1897 he took up painting in Munich, later visited Italy and North Africa and began exhibiting his early expressionist works. By 1910 he was influenced by Eastern thought; his paintings became non-figurative and he began his first book, which was translated into English as *The Art of Spiritual Harmony* (1914). In this he drew a parallel between painting and music and pointed out the difference between an impression (a direct pictorial rendering of something seen), an improvisation (a spontaneous arrangement of forms not necessarily related to nature), and a composition (a reasoned, slowly formed and carefully worked-over painting). He also analysed the spiritual significance of different colours, comparing them to the keyboard of an instrument. All this opened up immense new vistas, which have been extensively explored by later artists.

During the period 1910–20 Kandinsky's work was richly colourful and flowing in handling; after he left Russia in 1922 it became tight and geometrical, though still non-representational. His activity as Professor of Painting in Moscow was of short duration, but the theories he worked out there were afterwards applied at the Bauhaus in Germany. In this respect, as well as through his painting, he remains one of the key figures in the Russian contribution to modern art.

New movements followed each other in such rapid succession during these fertile years that it is difficult to see them all in their proper perspective. In 1913 KASIMIR MALEVICH (1878–1935) laid another foundation stone in the structure of abstract art by exhibiting the first of his "Squares". Later he coined the word "Suprematism", by which he wished to convey the supremacy of pure sensibility in art. He declared that external appearance was of no interest to the artist, only the feelings aroused by it had meaning. Therefore he sought pure expression without representation. Could the milk bottle, he asked, be the symbol of milk? His early work was Fauve in character, and he painted country scenes resembling some of Goncharova's. In about 1911 he became interested in Cubism and developed a tubular form of simplification akin to Léger's. Then followed the Squares, "Black on White", "Black and Red", "White on White" (1918, Museum of Modern Art, New York). Some of the more complex Suprematist compositions may have been suggested by the first sight of the world from an aircraft. In 1919 Malevich ousted Chagall from the Art School at Vitebsk and began to concentrate on putting his theories into writing. In 1927 he visited Germany, published his book *The Non-objective World* and left there a body of his work which is now in Amsterdam. After his return to Russia he was obliged to confine himself to portraiture.

The last original movement to arise in Russia was Constructivism. The architects of this were VLADIMIR TATLIN (1885–1953), ANTON PEVSNER (1886–1962) and his younger brother NAUM, who changed his name to GABO (b. 1890), and ALEXANDER RODCHENKO (1891–1956). Tatlin had begun making painted reliefs, constructions and assemblages of various materials already before 1914. During the first World War, Pevsner and Gabo were working in Oslo and they began to make similar experiments when they returned to Russia after the Revolution. A new theory propagated at the time was that art should be functional and closely allied to production. The projects designed by some of these artists, though never realized, are of the greatest interest, such as Tatlin's "Monument to the Third International" and Gabo's "Project for a Radio Station" (both 1919–20). The work they did for the theatre made a great impact, and perhaps the most lasting influence of these new ideas can be seen in typography and advertising, in which both Rodchenko and EL LISITSKII (1890–1941) excelled.

By 1922 these experimental tendencies began to be discredited in Russia. The artists who were unable to leave the country had to adapt their work to the new demand for social realism or produce designs for applied art. A sufficient number, however, settled in various countries in the West to bring over a salutary influence of original invention and make the rich flavour of the Russian artistic tradition known to the outside world.

CHAPTER VI

Soviet Art: 1917–1963

THE FIRST generation of Soviet painters had all received their training and formed their style before the Revolution. As the previous decade had been a period of exceptionally rapid change and development, they had followed a wide variety of tendencies. Some, like Arkhipov and Kasatkin, were survivors of the *Peredvizhniki;* this was to become the style most highly favoured in official circles, and consequently they have been extolled above their merits as artists for depicting the working classes in the spirit of Socialist Realism. Others, like KONSTANTIN YUON (1875–1958) and BORIS KUSTODIYEV (1878–1927), belonged to the "World of Art" group, but adapted their style with ease to the new requirements, because their interest had always been mainly with the people. They preferred to portray the more colourful aspects of the past, such as popular festivals at which national costumes were still worn, or life in remote parts of the country where old customs survived (Plate 30). Both these artists had absorbed the Impressionist theory of light and pure colour, but with a strong decorative bias, and their work stands out vividly among paintings by some of their rather drab contemporaries.

After studying at the Academy, Kustodiyev assisted Repin in painting the huge "Council of State", as well as doing a number of other portraits, but eventually turned his attention to compositions of provincial markets and holidays. His "Carnival Week" was exhibited at the Royal Academy in 1959, and became a popular Christmas card in England. After the Revolution, Kustodiyev painted some topical subjects, such as "The

Bolshevik", a giant carrying a red banner and striding over the buildings of Moscow. He was also a successful designer in the field of book illustration and for the theatre.

Yuon's interest lay mainly in recording the changing seasons in the countryside (Plate 18), and the picturesque architecture of old Russian cities. He, too, did work for the theatre, excelled as a black-and-white artist and, in later years, painted industrial landscapes and parades in Red Square.

Pure landscape has not altered much in character in the last half century. The formula of Levitan, Serov and of the more popular painters of the nineteenth century is still followed by Soviet artists, who do not seem to have developed any novelties of approach. The picture by ARKADII RYLOV (1870–1939), "In Blue Space", painted in 1918 and representing swans flying over the sea, has been hailed as the first expression of the new sense of freedom and the joyous outlook brought about by the Revolution (Plate 32). The treatment here is bold and effective. On the other hand, the picture known as "Transport coming back to normal", painted in 1923 by BORIS YAKOVLEV (b. 1890), may well have had a deep significance for the people who remembered the post-revolutionary chaos, but for anyone else it is merely a study of smoke and atmosphere such as was first attempted by Claude Monet in his "Gare St. Lazare" of 1877, which was an exciting novelty at the time.

YURII PIMENOV (b. 1903), has tried to reflect the new pattern of life in Soviet Russia by painting skyscrapers, city transport, and building operations in a slight, suggestive manner, but with none of the originality to be found in Nevinson's earlier inter-pretations of the new sensations of driving or flying. Pimenov came to London in 1961 to paint the sets for the Festival Hall production of *The Snow Maiden* and has recorded his impressions of England in a series of drawings.

In Russia, as in England, the influence of Cézanne was at its height in the twenties. At that time a number of painters who had had the advantage of studying in Paris were still working in

Russia. The heavy modelling and rich colour of PETR KONCHA-LOVSKII (1876–1956) recall the work of Duncan Grant. A new conception of plasticity was in the air at the time, and it was those painters who had experimented with Cubism, however slightly, who were best able to express themselves in this manner. Konchalovskii had studied in Paris in the late nineties and continued to work there periodically until 1914. He visited Italy and Spain and became thoroughly familiar with the modern trends of the day. His preoccupation with "formalism" has been denounced by Soviet art-historians, but it is, nevertheless, this factor that gives force and distinction to his subsequent work. The same is true of ILYA MASHKOV (1881–1944), who was even more revolutionary in his young days when he exhibited with the "Golden Fleece"; his later, well-constructed still-life compositions stand out for their tactile values and solidity. PAVEL KUZNETSOV (b. 1878) was another pioneer of the modern movement, he continued to work in a more conventional, though highly sensitive style.

A very different group of painters, active at the time of the Revolution, were painting in a more precise manner with emphasis on line. Of these KUZ'MA PETROV-VODKIN (1878–1939) was the first to spring to prominence and was given a studio at the Academy of Art in 1918. His large over life-size heads painted in blue monochrome, perhaps an echo of Picasso's blue period, intrigued the art students, who flocked to study under him. His picture "The Alarm" expresses anxious moments of the civil war, when houses were raided and sudden arrests made, but the dramatic subject does not preclude an attention to detail which is lacking in most of the younger Soviet painters. ISAAK BRODSKII (1884–1939) also achieves his realistic effects by intense particularization, so that many of his landscapes recall Brueghel. He too had studied in Western Europe and met Gor'kii in Italy; he is best known for his pictures of "Lenin in Smolnyi" and "Voroshilov on Skis"; a collection of his works is on view at the museum which now occupies his former studio in the Arts Square, Leningrad.

The most impressive picture evoked by the Revolution is "The Defence of Petrograd", painted in 1928 by ALEXANDER DEINEKA (b. 1899). The steel-like precision in the painting of the bridge and the sharp characterization in the lean, determined faces of the workers darkly silhouetted against a light background make it a memorable record of a historical event. The process of stylization and simplification seemed to point the way to the emergence of a new style appropriate to a new type of subject, but this never materialized. Deineka's own later work became lifeless and academic, as for example his "Relay Race", 1935 (Plate 35).

Soviet art historians claim that the new Soviet style reached full maturity in the thirties. Artists began to concentrate on prescribed subjects, such as the development of industry, the work of collective farms and historical scenes of the Revolution itself. After the invasion of Russia by the Germans in 1941 there was a great upsurge of patriotic feeling, and every means was employed to stimulate this, even to the extent of allowing subject matter to be taken from earlier Russian history. The enormous success of Eisenstein's film *Alexander Nevskii* resulted in the same subject being chosen for the decoration of one of the Moscow Metro Stations. The artist was PAVEL KORIN (b. 1892), who is descended from generations of ikon painters. He began his studies in the village of Palekh and continued them later in the Moscow School of Painting, where he worked under Nesterov. His figure of Alexander Nevskii, a warrior saint in armour, defending Novgorod against the Teutonic Knights has become the embodiment of the national hero. In his portraits Korin has recorded many celebrated contemporaries, including Gor'kii, Nesterov, Sar'yan and the sculptor Konenkov. Although his characterization is powerful and his colour tends to be sombre, the result is always a work of art and bears none of the superficial, photographic qualities of so many Soviet portraits. Korin has rendered valuable service in the preservation and restoration of ikon painting.

Another important personality in this field was the art historian

IGOR' GRABAR' (1871–1960). He studied first at the Academy under Repin, and later in Munich. He was a member of the "World of Art" group, began writing the first complete history of Russian art, and painted a number of delightful impressionist landscapes, which ranged from glittering snow scenes to sunny green meadows and trees. SERGEI GERASIMOV (b. 1885) works in a somewhat similar style and is much loved for his sensitive, typically Russian landscapes.

Among the younger landscape painters GEORGII NISSKII (b. 1903) has been more experimental in his choice of aspect—wide horizons, linear emphasis and strong colour distinguish him from the Impressionist painters. The older painter ARKADII PLASTOV (b. 1893), who specializes in representing the work of collective farms, endeavours to attain an air of modernity by using vivid colours and a broad brush-stroke, but his conception is still that of the nineties. The same is true of his contemporaries, the KUKRYNIKSY—three painters, Kupriyanov, Krylov and Sokolov; these have worked jointly under this pseudonym since their student days and now excel in satirical and political caricatures and such themes as "The Flight of the Capitalist" and "The End", which depicts the last minutes of Hitler and his generals in the bunker.

One of the features of modern Soviet art is the encouragement given to the peripheral Republics to develop their own national characteristics, and there is often more originality to be found in the outlying areas. Even the artists of Leningrad have a style of their own. In Kiev the distinguished painter TAT'YANA YABLON-SKAYA (b. 1917) has won fame with her huge canvas of women gathering grain and the delightful winter scene "Twins" (Plate 34). Her paintings express a mood of strength and happiness and are obviously painted with enjoyment. A number of Latvian painters specialize, appropriately enough, in pictures of the sea and fishing, while the veteran Armenian painter, MARTIROS SAR'YAN (b. 1880), paints the sun-drenched valleys and moun-tains of his native land (Plate 33). In his young days he was a pioneer of modernism, a member of the "Blue Rose" group, and the influence of the Fauves is still discernible in his colour-saturated still-life compositions and broadly conceived landscapes. Similarly SEMEN CHUIKOV (b. 1902) paints the people and mountains of Kirgizia freshly and vigorously.

The most famous piece of sculpture produced in the Soviet period is the huge "Factory Worker and Land Girl" by VERA MUKHINA (1889–1953). It was first shown at the Paris Exhibition of 1937, when it surmounted the Soviet Pavilion, and now stands near the entrance to the Exhibition of Economic Achievement in Moscow. Having studied under Yuon and Mashkov, and then in Paris in 1912–14, Mukhina mastered the new tendencies of that creative period as well as the classical traditions of French and Italian sculpture. Her early work, done during the Revolutionary period, was highly stylized, and it was not until the middle thirties that she succeeded in clothing her inherently plastic conceptions with the semblance of naturalness.

Quality of a more restrained kind appears in the work of the portrait sculptor NIKOLAI ANDREYEV (1873–1932). He devoted the last years of his life to a special study of Lenin and has recorded him in many characteristic aspects. SERGEI KONENKOV (b. 1874) belongs to the same generation and is honoured as the veteran Soviet sculptor. He has produced portrait busts as well as various schemes of decorative sculpture. After working in Western Europe and America from 1924–45, Konenkov returned to Russia and was awarded the Lenin Prize in 1957 for his magnificent "Self Portait" (Plate 31). Another outstanding sculptor, IVAN SHADR (1887–1941), a native of the Ural region, studied in Paris in 1910–12 and achieved great success in the early days of the Revolution with his figures of a "Worker", a "Red Army Soldier" and a "Peasant", which were widely reproduced on paper money and stamps. For the tenth anniversary of the Revolution he made his best known work, a nude youth lifting a paving stone, entitled "A Stone was the Weapon of the Proletariat in 1905". The demand for public monuments and portrait busts has been enormous since the Revolution, and it is not surprising that the general level of such sculpture is far below these few outstanding examples.

It is only in the graphic arts and in certain branches of applied art that inventiveness is allowed some scope, perhaps because from their very nature these art-forms cannot be as representational as painting. From VLADIMIR FAVORSKII (b. 1886), the oldest and most distinguished wood-engraver, to ANDREI USHIN (b. 1927), one of a host of younger engravers, Russia has produced an array of masters whose work finds a ready sale among private individuals (Plate 36). The limitations of the material impose a certain stylization through which the artist can express the poetry he is illustrating or his own mood, and the simpler the medium, the more effective becomes his endeavour to utilize its possibilities to the full.

In the presence of such obvious examples of talent, why is it that Soviet art is on the whole so uninspiring?

In every country there is a gulf between academic art, which satisfies the requirements for official portraits and conventional decorations on the one hand, and the more experimental tendencies, from which the living tradition usually emerges, on the other. The difference between the works shown in the Paris Salon and in the galleries on the left bank, or between the Royal Academy and the exhibitions sponsored by the Arts Council, prove that in Western Europe there is room for conformity as well as experiment. The fact that in the Soviet Union there seems to be no outlet for artists except in the approved convention must be crippling to the young and produces an output of dreary monotony. Socialist Realism as practised in other countries, for instance by the Italian Renato Guttuso or the American Ben Shahn, is far more vital than anything to be seen in Russia.

No bright star appears to have arisen in the Soviet art world since the war. Rumour has it that interesting work is being done by young artists and can be found in private collections, but it is certainly not apparent in the museums or public buildings and any attempt to exhibit it receives official rebuke. However, for those artists who conform to the current requirements, living conditions appear to be exceptionally good. All artists belong to the Union of Soviet Artists. This arranges exhibitions, promotes sales, determines prices, provides studios, rest and holiday homes, owns large factories producing artists' materials—in fact looks after the interests of its members in a way not to be found in any other country. Moreover, the public interested in art is far wider in Russia than anywhere else. It is only necessary to look at the crowds attending museums and exhibitions to realize how much remains to be done in this respect in the West. In the Soviet Union groups of workers are brought to museums, and works of art are taken to the factories, collective farms and schools. Books on art are eagerly sought after and go out of print with astonishing rapidity. All this suggests that the policy of bringing art to the masses is indeed bearing fruit. Perhaps, in order to achieve this wide dissemination of a taste for art, it was necessary to simplify the problem by admitting only the most obvious, easily understood type of painting in the first instance. At a later stage discrimination may develop and more originality may be tolerated; for surely the aim of socialism must be not to bring art down to the level of the workers' taste but rather to elevate the taste of the workers to the highest standards of beauty. Meanwhile, although so much is done to stimulate interest in art, the emphasis is always on subject rather than treatment, on the literary rather than on the visual approach to painting. Hardly a book or article appears without some warning against the dangers of "formalism", and since imagination and experiment are not encouraged, the field open to the artist is narrow and the style necessarily old-fashioned. It is indeed strange that in this space-age, when the U.S.S.R. has assumed the lead in scientific achievement, there should be no echo of new experiences and sensations in the visual arts. If painting were given the freedom and well-directed encouragement enjoyed by science, there is every chance that Russia would again be as close to the summit in art as she was at the time of the Revolution.

The Transliteration of Russian Words

RUSSIAN names and other words mentioned in the text have been transliterated automatically with no attempt to give a phonetic rendering. Exceptions have been made, at the author's discretion, in the case of names already familiar in some other spelling to readers in the West. A list of these is given below; forms in brackets are transliterations given for the benefit of readers who may wish to look up the names in Russian texts.

TRANSLITERATION TABLE

Russian Letter	Transliteration	Russian Letter	Transliteration
А	a	П	p
Б	b	Р	r
В	v	С	s
Г	g	Т	t
Д	d	У	u
Е	ye	Ф	f
	initially and after a vowel	Х	kh
	other than ы; *otherwise* e	Ц	ts
Ж	zh	Ч	ch
З	z	Ш	sh
И	i	Щ	shch
Й	i	Ъ	— (*none*)
К	k	Ы	y
Л	l	Ь	' (*apostrophe*)
М	m	Э	e
Н	n	Ю	yu
О	o	Я	ya

Exceptions

Chagall	(Shagal)
Chaliapin	(Shalyapin)
Diaghilev	(D'yagilev)
Gay	(Ge)
Kandinsky	(Kandinskii)
Mussorgsky	(Musorgskii)
Rimsky-Korsakov	(Rimskii-Korsakov)
Stanislavsky	(Stanislavskii)

Editor

Suggestions for Further Reading

(*Only works in English are listed: where not otherwise indicated,
the books are published in London.*)

ALPATOV, M. *The Russian Impact on Art* (Philosophical Library,
New York). 1950.

ARTS COUNCIL. *A Retrospective Exhibition of Paintings and
Designs for the Theatre: Larionov and Goncharova.* 1961.

BEAUMONT, CYRIL W. *Ballet Design Past and Present* (Studio).
1946.

BENOIS, A. *The Russian School of Painting* (T. Werner Laurie).
1916.

BUCKLE, RICHARD. *In Search of Diaghilev* (Sidgwick and Jackson).
1955.

BUNT, C. *Russian Art from Scyths to Soviets* (Studio). 1946.

CHEN, JACK. *Soviet Art and Artists* (Pilot Press). 1944.

CONWAY, MARTIN. *Art Treasurers of Soviet Russia* (Edward
Arnold). 1925.

ERBEN, WALTER. *Marc Chagall* (Thames and Hudson). 1957.

FARBMAN, M. (Editor). *Masterpieces of Russian Painting* (Europa).
1930.

FIALA, VLADIMIR. *Russian Painting.* (Prague). 1956.

GRAY, CAMILLA. *The Great Experiment* (Thames and Hudson).
1962.

GROHMANN, WILL. *Wassily Kandinsky* (Thames and Hudson).
1959.

HAMILTON, G. H. *The Art and Architecture of Russia* (Penguin
History of Art). 1954.

HASKELL, A. H. *The Russian Genius in Ballet* (Pergamon Press, Oxford). 1963.

HOLME, C. G. *Art in the U.S.S.R.* (Studio). 1935.

KANDINSKY, W. *Concerning the Spiritual in Art* (Witten Corn Schultz Inc., New York). 1947.

KELLY, LADY M. H. *A Mirror to Russia* (Country Life). 1951.

KELLY, LADY M. H. *A Picture Book of Russia* (Country Life). 1952.

KONDAKOV, N. P. *The Russian Icon* (Clarendon Press, Oxford). 1927.

LAZAREV, VIKTOR. *Andrei Rublev* (Moscow). 1960.

LAZAREV, VIKTOR. *Russian Icons* (UNESCO). 1958.

LOUKOMSKY, G. *History of Modern Russian Painting* (Hutchinson). 1945.

MARSDEN, C. *Palmyra of the North* (Faber and Faber). 1941.

NEWMARCH, ROSA. *The Russian Arts* (Herbert and Jenkins). 1916.

RICE, D. TALBOT. *Russian Art* (Gurney and Jackson, Edinburgh). 1935.

RICE, D. TALBOT. *Russian Icons* (King Penguin). 1947.

RICE, TAMARA TALBOT. *Russian Art* (Pelican Books). 1949.

RICE, TAMARA TALBOT. *A Concise History of Russian Art* (Thames and Hudson). 1963.

ROYAL ACADEMY OF ARTS. *Catalogue of an Exhibition of Works by Russian and Soviet Artists.* 1959.

RUBISSOV, HELEN. *The Art of Russia* (Philosophical Library, New York). 1946.

Guides to the Russian Museum (Leningrad), the Tret'yakov Gallery (Moscow) and certain other museums are available in English, as well as a number of monographs on Russian artists published by the Foreign Languages Publishing House, Moscow.

Index